The Linen
Cloths

...Jesus left behind

Books by Michael L.Dourson

Evidence of Faith Series
Messiah's Star
The Beginning
The Linen Cloths

The Linen Cloths

...Jesus left behind

MICHAEL L. DOURSON

Table of Contents

Preface

<hr>

*If Christ has not been raised, then our
preaching is in vain and your faith is in vain.
(<u>Corinthians 15:13</u>)*

This story is about the Shroud of Turin. This Shroud
and its related cloth or napkin, the Sudarium of Oviedo,
are reputed to be the burial cloths of Jesus of Nazareth.[1]
Parts of this story are based on Biblical narrative
(Revised Standard Version), primarily text from the
New Testament. Other parts are based on scientific
evidence that, for example, place these burial cloths to
the specific location of Jerusalem from an analysis of
soil, to the month of April from an analysis of pollen,
and to a year in the first century AD from a historical
and fabric analysis. Radioactive carbon dating is not
supportive of a first century date, but this dating is
controversial.[2] Still other parts of this story are based on
conversations, some of them hypothetical, among
various Biblical characters, including Jesus and his
apostles and disciples; Simon of Cyrene; Mary, the

mother of Jesus; and various antagonists during the last week of Jesus' life. The hypothetical conversations have been invented to fill in the Biblical narrative while honoring the Biblical and scientific contexts.

This story is intended to be complete, but however intended, it will likely not include all pertinent facts, and several of its interpretations will likely be improved or changed with further thought and discussion. As with any attempt at understanding the Shroud, several assumptions are made. First, it is assumed that the natural law (Nature) and the written law (the Bible) have the same dignity and teach the same things in a way that one of them has nothing more and nothing less than the other because they have the same author— God (St. Augustine, 354–430). It follows from such an assumption that both the Bible and Nature need to be studied in order to gain insights into the Shroud. Second, it is assumed that the inspired word of the Bible, in its various translations, reflects what actually happened, but using words that were most appropriate at the time of writing.

The story of the Shroud is important from a Christian perspective because it shows what appears to be a negative image of a male, crucified in an unusual way that may have occurred in the first century AD.

This image is not a forgery of any kind, not paint, not added substance, and not chemical administration. Rather, the image is formed by a change to the individual fibers of cloth that surrounded the body of this male. This change is not found on what would have been the outside fibers of the Shroud. Science cannot explain this change by any of its normal methods of analysis, although a radiation event has been hypothesized.[3]

So is the Shroud the cloth that enveloped the body of Jesus of Nazareth? Much has been written about this, and the interested soul is encouraged to dig deeper into one or more of the underlying issues. Alternatively, one can take the minimalist approach and state the hypothesis most likely to be correct, given the known facts.[4] This story takes the latter approach and weaves together three lines of evidence: scriptural, historical, and scientific.

End Notes

[1] See John 19:6–7.

[2] Wikipedia offers a balanced discussion of the available evidence and the associated uncertainties and controversies, and includes a wealth of references for additional reading. See https://en.wikipedia.org/wiki/Shroud_of_Turin.

[3] See for example, Mouraviev (1997) at https://www.Shroud.com/pdfs/mouraviev.pdf. However, this has also been questioned. See for example, Rogers (2005) at https://www.Shroud.com/pdfs/rogers8.pdf. Finally, see also The Shroud: Critical summary of observations, data and hypotheses. Version 3.0. The Shroud Center of

Colorado. 2015, page 71.
[4] See for example, T. Casabianca, "The Shroud of Turin: A Historiographical Approach", The Heythrop Journal, 54, 3, 2013, pages 414-423.

Chapter 1

The Crime Scene

I glorified thee on earth, having accomplished the work which thou gavest me to do; and now, Father, glorify thou me in thy own presence with the glory which I had with thee before the world was made. (John 17: 4–5 RSV)

Turin, Italy 1978

A middle-aged scientist, on leave from the NASA JPL imaging lab, collapsed into the folding chair at 3 a.m. in the morning. This was not his only rest in the last several days, but it was perhaps long enough to ask himself how he felt about the image of the crime scene. He had only a short time left to study and sample the image or perhaps a picture on the cloth.

Picture! What an odd thought, he mused. Several, perhaps many, of his colleagues who were part of this investigation were convinced before they arrived in Turin, Italy that the image had been painted on the cloth in the Middle Ages, that it was a clever forgery. It did not take very long, however, to disprove this speculation. And the growing belief among his fellow investigators, stated in snatches of moments between intense activity, was that the cloth from the crime scene was indeed a picture, actually a negative image from which a picture could be, and had been, developed over a hundred years ago.

None of his colleagues had a good hypothesis about how this negative image had come about, although several had been suggested and discarded. The owners of the relic were convinced that the image was part of a resurrection event—whatever that meant scientifically. But they were not able to explain the image either.

He momentarily forgot his specific assignment and looked at the cloth as a whole. It was a 14-foot, rectangular piece of fine linen,[5] about 3 feet wide, on which the image of both the front and back of a man was seen. The man's head had been placed in the middle of the linen with his feet to one end, so that when the linen was folded over the man's head, it completely covered him, with the loose ends of the folded part of the linen covering his feet. Interestingly, while the image of this individual was evident on the open part of this cloth, when the cloth was closed there was no readily apparent image on the outside.

However, something did not seem right, or maybe it was just the hour of the day. It was clearly evident that the body shown in the image was horribly mutilated—

and it showed this mutilation on both the front and backside of the man in the image. Scourge marks made by a Roman flagrum,[6] profuse bleeding at multiple points, especially around the head, and spike marks evident in the wrists and feet, clearly showed a crucifixion. A gouge of blood in the side of the torso showed what could easily have been a spear thrust, as the owners of the relic insisted it was. The pain associated with the brutal torture and execution of the man shown in this linen must have been extreme.

He carefully focused on the scene again, and this time noted that in contrast to the body that was terribly beat up, the face looked serene.[7] Despite Roman torture that would leave even the strongest man whimpering, the face of the man belied what the marks on his body plainly stated. The image of the body and the face on the cloth just did not go together.[8]

<hr>

Golgotha, Jerusalem, Israel, 3 p.m., 33 AD

It is finished. (John 19:30)

End Notes

[5] The Greek word used to describe the shroud in the

New Testament is sindōn, meaning "linen cloth, especially one which was fine and costly." See https://www.blueletterbible.org/lang/lexicon/lexicon.cfm?Strongs=G4616&t=RS.

[6] A flagrum is a whip, especially a multi-thong type, usually used for punishment by striking the backside of a human.

[7] See Appendix Figure 1.

[8] Statement of Dr. Donald Lynn as seen on the Jesus and the Shroud of Turin, TLC video. Questar. ISBN 1-56855-944-5.

Chapter 2

An Ancient Prophecy Fulfilled

Cyrene, North Africa, Autumn 29 AD

Simon of Cyrene a former apprentice of the magus, Gaspar of Babylon, was now a middle-aged man. He had a lovely wife, two sons, and a daughter, and was now the leading magus of the Temple of Zeus. His apprenticeship with Gaspar, more than thirty years ago, had been a good move when he was much younger. This experience had led to opportunities unavailable to other aspiring magi.

His life had proceeded smoothly, but he often wondered about the Jewish Messiah that Gaspar and his entourage from Babylon had visited in Bethlehem in the year 2 BC. Simon fervently believed the words that Gaspar had spoken to him after they had returned, that he, Simon, would somehow be a part of this Messiah's work. As he grew older, Simon had eagerly listened to any scrap of information out of Israel concerning the Messiah's possible activities. But as Simon matured in his career and family, his work was all consuming, and he heard nothing out of Israel...for twenty-nine years.

Then one day in the autumn of the year 29 AD, an exciting message was passed on to him by one of the merchants who routinely plied the Mediterranean Sea. A wild man in the Judean wilderness was baptizing people with water and asking the baptized to repent of their sins. This wild man–or was he really a prophet?— the merchant certainly thought so—was said to have boldly stated, when asked by the authorities if he was the Christ, "I am not the Christ.[9]" (John 1:20)

Perhaps this twenty-nine year silence actually reflects an appropriate length of time, Simon thought, especially because Jewish men are not considered spiritually mature until the age of thirty. This Jesus of Bethlehem, if he actually survived King Herod's slaughter of the innocent children in the year 1 BC, as Gaspar assured me he did, and if this Jesus is the Jewish Messiah, he would have turned thirty a few months earlier on June 17.[10]

During the spring of the following year, 30 AD, Simon received a report from Jerusalem of a disturbance in the Temple at Passover, where an itinerant rabbi called Jesus of Nazareth was said to have driven out all of the merchants from the courts of the temple. During the summer of 30 AD, Simon heard other reports of this Jesus who was healing the sick and casting out demons in Galilee. Could this be the same Jesus that I visited so many years ago in Bethlehem? Simon pondered.

Simon went back to the original prophecy of Daniel, in which Daniel wrote:

> *Seventy weeks of years are decreed concerning your people and your holy city, to finish the transgression, to put an end to sin, and to atone for iniquity, to bring in everlasting righteousness, to seal both vision and prophet and to anoint a most holy place. Know therefore and understand that from the going forth of the word to restore and build Jerusalem to the coming of an anointed one, a prince, there shall be seven weeks. Then for sixty-two weeks it shall be built again with square and moat, but in a troubled time. And after the sixty-two weeks, an anointed one shall be cut off, and shall have nothing, and the people of the prince who is to come shall destroy the city and the sanctuary. (Daniel 9:24–26)*

Simon remembered telling Gaspar his interpretation of this prophecy: If this is to be interpreted as seventy weeks of years between the building of our glorious city Jerusalem and the death of the anointed one, as directed for us to consider in Leviticus 25:8, then this would be 490 years. We know that the temple was rebuilt in the year of Ezra's commission in 3303 (458 BC), so it follows that the anointed one would be cut off, or killed, in the year 3793 (33 AD).[11]

As the year 30 AD progressed into 31, more stories

circulated about this man called Jesus of Nazareth, and Simon began to think that another visit to Jerusalem, but this time with his family, might be appropriate. He longed to see the Messiah again!

End Notes

[9] Christ and Messiah mean anointed or anointed one. The term Christ is an English derivative of the New Testament Greek word Christos, which means "anointed." See https://www.ucg.org/bible-study-tools/booklets/jesus-christ-the-real-story/what-do-messiah-and-jesus-christ-mean.

[10] See Appendix Figure 2 for the timelines of John the Baptist and Jesus of Nazareth. All dates in this story are given in our current modern calendar. But of course, our current calendar was not used in the time of Jesus.

[11] The author is indebted to the work of John Pratt for this synthesis (Meridian Magazine, 15 September, 2004).

Chapter 3

————◇————

My Time Has Not Yet Come

When the wine failed, the mother of Jesus said to him, "They have no wine." And Jesus said to her, "O woman, what have you to do with me? My hour has not yet come." (John 2:3–4)

Nazareth June 12 (Silvan 14), 29 AD

Jesus looked around at the carpentry shop, Joseph's shop actually. He had learned his trade from his foster father, Joseph, at a very young age. Joseph had lived until Jesus was in his early twenties and had given him not only a trade to carry on to make a living for him and his mother Mary, but also a human reverence for God, his creation, and his fellow humans.

Joseph had also given Jesus an understanding of human forbearance. More than once, Jesus overheard gossip that he, Jesus, was a bastard child, and that his true father was someone other than Joseph. The usual line of false reasoning was that Mary had met up with a younger man while she was visiting her aunt Elizabeth in a city of Judah while Elizabeth was pregnant. On all such occasions, Joseph gently insisted that the gossiper had this incorrect, that Jesus was God's child, and that the important thing to remember in the small-knit community of Nazareth was to not bear false witness against one's neighbor. All of this was instructive to Jesus.

Jesus had completed his one remaining carpentry task earlier in the day. He turned thirty years old that evening and the Spirit tugged at him. He smiled, looked around one more time and kissed the wood that still held the Creator's touch, his touch.

Mary called him for a celebration dinner. He walked out of the shop and closed the door.

Jordan River, June 15 (Silvan 17) of 29 AD

The next day Jesus had packed his few possessions, kissed his mother Mary goodbye, and left Nazareth on a 3-day journey to Judea, near the River Jordan, where his cousin John was baptizing. Coming to the river Jesus stood in line to be baptized.

John, finally seeing Jesus, was startled. He objected, saying, "I need to be baptized by you, and do you come to me?"

Jesus smiled and answered him, "Let it be so now for thus it is fitting for us to fulfill all righteousness."

So John relented. Jesus was baptized, and when he went up immediately from the water the heavens were opened and John saw the Spirit of God descending like a dove, and alighting on him. Then this same Spirit of God led Jesus into the wilderness to be tempted by the devil. And he fasted forty days and forty nights.[12]

Bethany beyond the Jordan, August of 29 AD

"Who are you?" the priests and Levites, sent from the Pharisees, asked once again.

"I am not the Christ," the wild-looking man with a garment of camel's hair and a leather girdle around his waist stated once again.[13]

"What then? Are you Elijah?"

"I am not."

"Are you the prophet?"

"No."

"Who are you? Let us have an answer for those who sent us. What do you say about yourself?" the learned men demanded.

"As I have said before," John spoke evenly, "I am the voice of one crying in the wilderness, 'Make straight the way of the Lord,' as the prophet Isaiah said."

"Then why are you baptizing, if you are neither the Christ, nor Elijah, nor the prophet?" the learned men sneered.

"I baptize with water, but among you stands one whom you do not know, even he who comes after me, the thong of whose sandal I am not worthy to untie," John replied.[14]

"What kinds of answers are these?" the learned men

asked each other. And getting no further information from John, they left him with his numerous disciples by the side of the Jordan River and went back to report to their leaders.

Several days later Jesus returned from the wilderness. John saw Jesus coming toward him, and said to his disciples:

> *Behold, the Lamb of God, who takes away the sin of the world! This is he of whom I said, "After me comes a man who ranks before me, for he was before me." I myself did not know him, but for this I came baptizing with water, that he might be revealed to Israel… But he who sent me to baptize with water said to me, "He on whom you see the Spirit descend and remain, this is he who baptizes with the Holy Spirit." And I have seen and have borne witness that this is the Son of God. (John 1:29–34)*

The next day John was standing with two of his disciples; he looked at Jesus walking nearby and said, to his disciples again, "Behold, the Lamb of God!" The two disciples, John and Andrew, heard him say this, and they followed Jesus. Jesus turned, saw them following, and said to them, "What do you seek?"

"Rabbi, where are you staying?"

Jesus said to them, "Come and see."

Andrew and John came and saw where Jesus was staying. John then stayed with Jesus and Andrew found his brother Simon and said to him, "We have found the

Messiah." Andrew brought Simon to Jesus.

Jesus looked at him and said, "So you are Simon, the son of John [the fisherman]?

"Yes," replied Simon.

Jesus answered, "You shall be called Cephas" (which means Peter).

The next day Jesus decided to return to Galilee. Along the way he found Philip and said to him, "Follow me." Phillip did, and along the way Philip found Nathanael and said to him, "We have found him of whom Moses in the law and also the prophets wrote, Jesus of Nazareth, the son of Joseph." All 5 of Jesus's new disciples followed Jesus to Galilee.[15]

Cana in Galilee, September of 29 AD

It was a lovely day, and Mary was going to a marriage feast in Cana,[16] which was not too distant a walk from her home with Jesus in Nazareth. As she walked, she remembered an earlier day in June of 2 BC,[17] where she had been betrothed to Joseph so many years ago, what was it, 31 years? The joy of that event and the joy of all the events that followed, including the arduous but safe journey to Bethlehem with Joseph when she was so heavily pregnant, the birth of Jesus on the night of a glorious conjunction of Venus and Jupiter, the spectacular tales of the shepherds about the visit of angels, the prophesies of Simeon and Anna on the day of Mary's purification ceremony, the visit several months later of the magi and their entourage—and the excitement of Gaspar's apprentice, Simon—all these memories made Mary smile.

But as the prophet Simeon had also foretold, Mary's soul had been troubled, too.[18] The nighttime trip to Egypt to protect Jesus and then back to Nazareth was not easy. And the horrible story of the murder of all Bethlehem baby boys, many of them sons of mothers she had come to know in her short time in Bethlehem, left her weeping.

Jesus had stayed with Mary in Nazareth after Joseph died. He continued on with the carpenter's trade, but more and more, he had been out and about preparing himself for his Father's work. As she walked to the wedding feast, Mary recalled that Jesus had been about his Father's work since his childhood. He had gone missing for three days after the Passover feast when he was only twelve years old, and when she asked, "Son, why have you treated us so? Behold, your father and I have been looking for you anxiously" he answered in a way that neither she nor Joseph understood at that time, "How is it that you sought me? Did you not know that I must be in my Father's house?"[19]

Coming back to the present, Mary realized that she was anxious about her son's recent whereabouts and hoped to see him at the wedding feast. She had heard of his spiritual testing, and realized that he probably would disclose some of the highlights only to her.

Arriving at Cana, Mary smiled. Jesus was there, along with five men who appeared to be disciples. He introduced them to her as John, Andrew, Peter, Philip, and Nathanael. She was not at all surprised that Jesus had started to attract disciples, some of whom even appeared to be former disciples of John, her nephew. After all, Mary thought, was Jesus not to be about his Father's business?

> *During the course of the celebration, the wine ran out. Mary sought out Jesus and said to him, "They have no wine." Jesus replied, "O woman, what have you to do with me? My hour has not yet come."* [20] *[Mary] turned to the servants and said, "Do whatever he tells you." (John 2:2–5)*

Jesus inwardly sighed. Although ready to start his ministry, his cousin John was in full stride, preparing his way. Jesus was content for now to carefully select his disciples rather than to demonstrate signs for the kingdom, and it might be premature to reveal himself before John's work was finished. However, realizing that his mother had given him a way to keep his actions quiet by enlisting the help of only the servants, he smiled at her. Yes, he thought to himself, I will be obedient to my mother.

Looking around, Jesus saw six stone jars standing close by for the Jewish rites of purification, each able to hold twenty or thirty gallons of water.[21] He said to the servants:

"Fill the jars with water." And they filled them up to the brim. He said to them, "Now draw some out, and take it to the steward of the feast." So they took it. When the steward of the feast tasted the water now become wine, and did not know where it came from (though the servants who had drawn the water knew), the steward of the feast called the bridegroom and said to him, "Every man serves the good wine first; and when men have drunk freely, then the poor wine; but you have kept the good wine until now." (John 2:7–10)

The wedding feast ended on a good note. Afterward, Jesus went down to Capernaum with his mother, his brothers, and his disciples, and there they stayed for a few days.[22]

Nazareth, Fall of 32 AD

Much had occurred during the time between the feast of Cana, where Jesus quietly performed his first miracle, and the upcoming feast of Tabernacles. During the Passover of the year 30, Jesus had cleared the outer courts of the Jewish temple of trading activity in righteous anger with a whip of cords.[23] His cousin John had later been imprisoned and killed. However, Jesus continued to perform miracles, one of them particularly controversial during the Jewish Passover when he healed a paralyzed man on the Sabbath in 31AD.[24] And Jesus had preached good news to the poor, his fellow Jews, and even to the Samaritans.[25]

But he had been keeping most of his activity to the

area of Galilee since his healing of the paralyzed man. So his brothers said to him:

> *"Leave here and go to Judea [Jerusalem], that your disciples may see the works you are doing. For no man works in secret if he seeks to be known openly. If you do these things, show yourself to the world." For even his brothers did not believe in him. (John 7:2-5)*

Jesus pondered his brothers' words. They were correct to suggest that he should again preach openly in Judea near Jerusalem. But the two incidents in the Jewish temple were still fresh in the minds of many authorities, and Jesus had not gone to Judea again because they sought to kill him. So he said to his brothers:

> *"My time has not yet come,[26] but your time is always here. The world cannot hate you, but it hates me because I testify of it that its works are evil. Go to the feast yourselves; I am not going up to this feast, for my time has not yet fully come." (John 7:6–8)*

But after his brothers had gone up to the feast, Jesus also went up, not publicly but in private. After participating in the feast quietly for the first several days:

> *Jesus went up into the temple and taught. The Jews marveled at it, saying, "How is it*

that this man has learning, when he has never studied?"

So Jesus answered them, "My teaching is not mine, but his who sent me; if any man's will is to do his will, he shall know whether the teaching is from God or whether I am speaking on my own authority. He who speaks on his own authority seeks his own glory; but he who seeks the glory of him who sent him is true, and in him there is no falsehood. Did not Moses give you the law? Yet none of you keeps the law. Why do you seek to kill me?"

The people answered, "You have a demon! Who is seeking to kill you?"

Jesus answered them, "I did one deed [healing the invalid on the Sabbath at Passover of 31 AD], and you all marvel at it. Moses gave you circumcision (not that it is from Moses, but from the fathers), and you circumcise a man upon the Sabbath. If on the Sabbath a man receives circumcision, so that the law of Moses may not be broken, are you angry with me because on the Sabbath I made a man's whole body well? Do not judge by appearances, but judge with right judgment." [27]

Some of the people of Jerusalem therefore said, "Is not this the man whom they seek to kill? And here he is, speaking openly, and they say nothing to him! Can it be that the authorities really know that this is the Christ? Yet we know where this man comes from; and when the Christ appears, no one will know where he comes from."

So Jesus proclaimed, as he taught in the temple, "You know me, and you know where I come from? But I have not come of my own accord; he who sent me is true, and him you do not know. I know him, for I come from him, and he sent me.

They sought to arrest him;[28] but no one laid hands on him, because his hour had not yet come. Yet many of the people believed in him; they said, "When the Christ appears, will he do more signs than this man has done?" The Pharisees heard the crowd thus muttering about him, and the chief priests and Pharisees sent officers to arrest him. (John 7:14-32)

... but no one laid hands on him [then either]. The officers then went back to the chief priests and Pharisees, who said to them, "Why did you not bring him?"

The officers answered, "No man ever spoke like this man!"

The Pharisees answered them, "Are you led astray, you also? Have any of the authorities or of the Pharisees believed in him? But this crowd, who do not know the law, are accursed."

Nicode'mus, who had gone to [Jesus] before, and who was one of [the Pharisees], said to them, "Does our law judge a man without first giving him a hearing and learning what he does?"

They replied, "Are you from Galilee too? Search and you will see that no prophet is to rise from Galilee."

They went each to his own house, but Jesus went to the Mount of Olives. (John 7:44–53; John 8:1)

Early in the morning he came again to the temple; all the people came to him, and he sat down and taught them.

Again Jesus spoke to them, saying, "I am the light of the world; he who follows me will not walk in darkness, but will have the light of life."

The Pharisees then said to him, "You are bearing witness to yourself; your testimony is not true."

Jesus answered, "Even if I do bear witness to myself, my testimony is true, for I know whence I have come and whither I am going, but you do not know whence I come or whither I am going. You judge according to the flesh, I judge no one. Yet even if I do judge, my judgment is true, for it is not I alone that judge, but I and he who sent me. In your law it is written that the testimony of two men is true; I bear witness to myself, and the Father who sent me bears witness to me."

They said to him therefore, "Where is your Father?"

Jesus answered, "You know neither me nor my Father; if you knew me, you would know my Father also."

These words he spoke in the treasury, as he taught in the temple; but no one arrested him [a third time], because his hour had not yet come. (John 8:2; John 8:12–20)

Jerusalem, March of 33 AD

Winter had passed, but not without its tension. Jesus had again been tested multiple times during his participation at the feast of the Dedication at Jerusalem in the winter of 32 AD. The Jewish leadership was in suspense. Was Jesus going to claim to be the Messiah or not? Jesus' answers had left them puzzled and angry. Once again they had tried to kill or arrest him[29]

But now the feast of Passover was upon them. Jesus

was again in the Jerusalem area. He had raised Lazarus from the dead only a few short weeks before. News of this event was captivating and his presence at any place drew an instant crowd. The Jewish leadership was concerned with his popularity and for their place among the Jewish people and their Roman overlords.

Among those who went up to worship at the feast were some God fearing Greeks. Some of these worshipers came to Philip, and said to him, "Sir, we wish to see Jesus." Philip went and found Andrew and together they went and talked with Jesus. After introductions and during the course of discussion Jesus said:

> *The hour has [now] come for the Son of man to be glorified. Truly, truly, I say to you, unless a grain of wheat falls into the earth and dies, it remains alone; but if it dies, it bears much fruit. He who loves his life loses it, and he who hates his life in this world will keep it for eternal life. If any one serves me, he must follow me; and where I am, there shall my servant be also; if any one serves me, the Father will honor him. Now is my soul troubled. And what shall I say? 'Father, save me from this hour'? No, for this purpose I have come to this hour. (John 12:20–27)*

Jesus' time was now arriving. He had about one week left in his ministry. And the heavens above were also preparing to announce that Jesus' time had come with three signs.

End Notes

[12]The foregoing text was paraphrased from Matthew 3:13–16 and 4:1–2. The exact date of Jesus' baptism is inferred from an unusual conjunction of Saturn, the Jewish protectorate (in this case representing Jesus), and Mercury, God's messenger (in this case representing John), which occurred on June 15th of 29 (or Silvan 17 of the Jewish calendar). A travel time of 3 days from around Nazareth to this part of the Jordan river is implied in John 1:43 and John 2:1. For further discussion of celestial events as they relate to the life of Christ, please see my book about the Star of Bethlehem, Messiah's Star.

[13] See Matthew 3:4 for a description of John the Baptist's clothing and diet.

[14] The foregoing text was paraphrased from John 1:19–27.

[15] The foregoing text was paraphrased from John 1:29–45.

[16] Several locations of Cana have been proposed. The most likely candidate is Khirbet Cana, which is eight to nine miles from Nazareth. (See McCollough, 2015. Searching for Cana. Biblical Archaeology Review. Pages 31–39.) Little information exists regarding the time of year of this wedding feast. This story assumes that the feast was in the fall and that several months occurred between John 2:12 and John 2:13. Other interpretations are possible and should be explored.

[17] Messiah's Star, Chapter 2 and Appendix Table 1. The latter is found at http://messiahsstar.com/appendix-to-messiahs-star/

[18] See Luke 2:35.

[19] The suggestion that Jesus had been ready for his

ministry for a long time can be inferred from the following text found in Luke (2:41–51):

> *Now his parents went to Jerusalem every year at the feast of the Passover. And when he was twelve years old, they went up according to custom; and when the feast was ended, as they were returning, the boy Jesus stayed behind in Jerusalem. His parents did not know it, but supposing him to be in the company they went a day's journey, and they sought him among their kinsfolk and acquaintances; and when they did not find him, they returned to Jerusalem, seeking him. After three days they found him in the temple, sitting among the teachers, listening to them and asking them questions; and all who heard him were amazed at his understanding and his answers. And when they saw him they were astonished; and his mother said to him, "Son, why have you treated us so? Behold, your father and I have been looking for you anxiously." And he said to them, "How is it that you sought me? Did you not know that I must be in my Father's house?" And they did not understand the saying which he spoke to them. And he went down with them and came to Nazareth, and was obedient to them; and his mother kept all these things in her heart.*

[20] The statement of Jesus "My hour has not yet come" to Mary, his mother, in John 2:4 is of uncertain meaning. That she wanted him to perform a miracle seemed clear from the situation, and his response would also seem to be related to this potential miracle. Other references to Jesus' "hour" or "time" later in the Gospels is clearly

not associated with performing miracles. Rather such references appear to be associated with His eventual death. John the Baptist is arrested at some point after the miracle of changing the water into wine, and afterwards Jesus begins to preach (Matthew 4:12). At one time after the arrest of John, Jesus says: "Let us go on to the next towns, that I may preach there also; for that is why I came out." (Mark 1:38)

[21] The jars would likely be empty at this point in the feast since most, if not all of the guests had already arrived and gone through the purification rites.

[22] See John 2:12.

[23] See John 2:14–16.

[24] See John 5:8–16.

[25] See John 4:39–42.

[26] This is the second reference that the time of Jesus has not come. In the first instance at the wedding at Cana, his statement appears to be referring to prematurely starting his ministry. However, in this part of the narrative, Jesus is nearing the end of his ministry. Thus, he may be referring his death. Although other interpretations are possible, the heavens will soon unfold a series of 3 events that is very much tied to the time of death of Jesus as more fully described in the next chapter.

[27] An interesting commentary on this passage is found in The Jewish Gospel of John. Discovering Jesus, King of All Israel by Eli Lizorkin-Eyzenberg, Jewish Studies for Christians, Tel Aviv, Israel, 2015 page 125), specifically:

It is clear that Jesus was referring to his healing of a Jewish man at the Pool of Bethesda, which had occurred during his previous trip to Jerusalem. [The] pool in Hellenized Jerusalem very likely functioned as the healing sanctuary of Asclepius, the Greek god of medicine and health. This healing occurred on the Sabbath and it is likely that Jesus disturbed the public order by walking into a pagan facility and healing someone in the name of Israel's God. As we read, we must also understand that Jewish authorities worked under the watchful eye of Roman authority. The Roman Empire had its own values. Jewish beliefs were tolerated as long as they did not infringe on the pagan cults, and this was a case of infringement. Jesus, a Jewish religious leader, wielded his authority and power in the Asclepion. Both the Temple authorities and the Romans were very concerned. Therefore, in order to distance themselves from Jesus, the Temple authorities accused him of Sabbath desecration. The Ioudaioi's [Jewish leadership's] blind commitment to stop Jesus and strip him of his growing popularity closed their eyes to being able to see the obvious.

[28] The intent to arrest Jesus was likely because his reference to being sent from God the father.

[29] See John 10:22–39.

Chapter 4

The Sun, the Ram, and the Moon

Now before the feast of the Passover, when Jesus knew that his hour had come to depart out of this world to the Father, having loved his own who were in the world, he loved them to the end. (John 13:1)

Jerusalem, Thursday April 2, 33 AD

Jesus' day started, as all Jewish days started, with sundown on what would have been April 2, followed by a dinner with just his twelve disciples. The ensuing teachings to his disciples, betrayal by Judas for 30 pieces of silver, arrest by temple and Roman soldiers, abandonment by his disciples, trial and conviction by the Sanhedrin, display before Pilate and Herod, and then scourging, mocking, and sentencing by Pilate was a whirlwind that consumed the late evening and Thursday night and Friday morning.

———◇———

Jesus stumbled again.

"You," a guard sneered to a nearby spectator. "Yes, you with the two brats. Come here and help this man carry his crosspiece," the Roman soldier said with contempt. "He obviously does not have the strength to do it. Come quickly, before I drag you over here!"

The spectator, Simon of Cyrene,[30] started to ask the guard to pick someone else but then stopped as the man on the ground looked up.

"Simon," Jesus spoke from the ground, "please help me carry this."

Simon looked closely at the man. Profusely bleeding from wounds all over his body and a twisted, ugly row of thorns covering his head. How is this man even able to speak? Simon thought.

And then recognition set in. How does this man know my name?

"Yes, Lord," Simon responded and moved, now not reluctantly, to step in.

"Oh, yes, call him 'Lord'," barked the guard, "everyone else thinks this Jesus is the king of Israel. But be quick and pick up this crosspiece or I'll flog you instead."

Simon thought, How is it that this man—Jesus?—could even recognize him. The last time Simon was in Jerusalem was as Gaspar's assistant thirty-three years ago. Was this the same Jesus? If this was the Jesus of

Bethlehem, he was only six months old at the time of Simon's visit.

And through his disfigured face, Jesus smiled, "Simon, it is good to see you again; thank you for doing this for me..."

Jesus' statement sent a shock through Simon. He picked up Jesus and then his crosspiece. Scores of questions arose in his head, but he was unable to get any of them out of his mouth. Glancing back at his sons, Alexander and Rufus,[31] he motioned for them to keep up.

"...For otherwise I would not be able to fulfill the scriptures," Jesus continued.

"Yes, Lord," Simon replied. He really could not think of anything else to say, but felt satisfied when Jesus no longer needed help in standing up and walking forward.

———— ◇ ————

Judas stormed into the court of the chief priest, repenting, "I have sinned in betraying innocent blood." Taken back by this intrusion, Caiaphas retorted, "What is this to us? See to it yourself."[32]

Several of the attending scribes blanched at the priest's comment. Although it was certainly unusual for anyone to barge into the chambers of the chief priest, especially unannounced, Judas had been a guest of Caiaphas only just the previous evening, so his presence here was not strange and probably explained why he had not been stopped before he got here. However, what was strange was Caiaphas's comment. The response of any priest to a confession of sin would be to prescribe an appropriate sacrifice, and in the case of innocent blood, a hefty fine. As the chief priest, Caiaphas certainly knew this.

Judas gasped. His own priest refused his repentance. He threw down his payment for the betrayal of Jesus and stormed out in despair. Caiaphas motioned for the thirty pieces of silver to be picked up. "It is not lawful to put them into the treasury, since they are blood money. Let us use this to purchase a burial field."[33] A scribe noted the request and arranged for the money to be stored away from the treasury until an appropriate purchase could be made.

After lunch, Caiaphas and his father-in-law, Annas, went to Golgotha in the gathering gloom to witness the crucifixion of Jesus of Nazareth. As usual, they were surrounded by their entourage of attendants, but as their carriages moved along, the usually obsequious crowd was silent, with many folks weeping[34] and some individuals were actually rude. "Look," shouted someone from the crowd, "here are our chief priests and rulers [who] delivered him up to be condemned to death, and crucified him!"[35]

Annas was vaguely unsettled by the comment, but Caiaphas simply chuckled. "Your plan worked brilliantly, Father. The Roman governor, Pilate, quickly capitulated when you mentioned his political situation. He had no response but to give in. I sometimes wonder who really is in charge here."

Annas smiled at his son in law's words. Yes, his plan had worked well, almost too well, in fact. And that the crowds were not in their usual character really did not bother him. They would get over this Jesus in short order. But then why am I still ill at ease, he thought, it must be this infernal darkness. What kind of heavenly darkness is this?[36]

As they moved forward and the light failed, Annas had a recollection of a previous Day of Atonement, when he, as high priest at the time, had officiated. On this day he had conducted the yearly ceremony of taking two identical and blemish-free goats.[37] He had cast a lot to choose which of the two goats was to be for the Lord and the other, a scapegoat, to bear the collective sins of the people. After having designated each of the goats, he let go the scapegoat, the one with sin, to wander in the wilderness, and then killed the goat for the Lord, the one without sin, to atone for the sins of Israel. And why have I thought about this? the ever-analytic Annas asked himself.

The crucifixion was a sorry affair, and Annas and Caiaphas arrived just in time to see the Roman soldiers raising Jesus up and for Jesus to say, "Father, forgive them, for they know not what they do."[38] Annas actually had a brief pang of guilt for this Jesus because he had never heard reports of Jesus doing anything personally wrong, at least not before his obvious blasphemy earlier in the morning. But not all of the Sanhedrin thought that Jesus' response was blasphemy. "But what if he is the Messiah?" Nicode'mus had exclaimed. "Would the Messiah do yet more stunning miracles than raising Lazarus of Bethany from the dead just last month?" But many of the council muttered that this was just a stunt. Annas caught himself in this reminiscence and forcefully redirected his thinking to the reason for his scheme, that this man's life was being forfeited for Israel. He recalled his son-in-law Caiaphas's words when arguing among the Jewish leadership earlier in the week that:

> You do not understand that it is expedient for you that one man should die for the people, and that the whole nation should not perish. (John 11:50)

Jesus hung naked between two thieves. His garments had already been divided—by lot, no doubt, Annas thought. The thieves were harassing him. His body had been beaten severely. He was bleeding profusely. And the paid crowd was hurling the expected insults. Caiaphas then added his:

> He saved others; he cannot save himself. He is the king of Israel; let him come down from the cross and we will believe in him. He trusts in God; let God deliver him now, if he desires him: for he said, "I am the Son of God." (Matthew 27:41–43)

36

Several others of the priestly entourage also joined in.

Annas remained silent in thought and then the answer to his previous self-question came to him in a rush. Two men were displayed before Pilate that very morning: Jesus Barabbas and Jesus of Nazareth. No one questioned the fact that Jesus Barabbas was a miserable sinner, but he was nevertheless let go to wander in the wilderness of his sins. This left Jesus of Nazareth, the very Jesus whose execution he was now observing, and Caiaphas's words now sounded very different, "that one man should die for the people, and that the whole nation should not perish." Annas's plan of redeeming Israel by killing this Jesus, the very plan that was now unfolding before his eyes so very well, almost too well, seemed now somehow warped.

This is just happenstance, Annas thought, the goats from the Day of Atonement have nothing to do with these two men both called Jesus. But his previous unease turned to mild nausea, and then the sky became even darker.

Everyone became quiet.

"Lord, please remember me when you come into your kingdom," blurted out the thief on his right, his strength failing.

"I say to you truly, today you will be with me in paradise," Jesus responded.[39]

Sometime later the light failed, and only dim shadows could be made out. Jesus cried, "My God, my

God, why hast thou forsaken me?

Caiaphas chuckled, "Wonderful," he said loudly to Annas and their entourage, "his disciples will never be able to live down this statement. He is calling to his God and has been abandoned. The Messiah would never have done this."

But Annas had gasped at Jesus' words and then whispered to Caiaphas, "You fool, do you not know your scripture?"[40]

"Whatever do you mean, Annas?" Caiaphas replied.

"This Jesus of Nazareth is quoting Psalm 22. Do I need to rehearse this for you?"

"But what has this appropriate execution have to do with that prayer?" retorted Caiaphas more sternly.

"Look around, Caiaphas. What do you see?"

"A lot of blood and not much else; this infernal darkness is unnerving. Let's go." Caiaphas was now furious. Several members of their entourage had heard the exchange.

"Yes, we will go," replied Annas more loudly, "but not before I rehearse the psalm for you and the rest of our group." Annas continued:

> *My God, my God, why hast thou forsaken me? Why art thou so far from helping me, from the words of my groaning? O my God, I cry by day, but thou dost not answer; and by night, but find no rest. Yet thou art holy, enthroned on the praises of Israel. In thee our fathers trusted; they trusted, and thou didst deliver them. To thee they cried, and were saved; in*

thee they trusted, and were not disappointed. But I am a worm, and no man; scorned by men, and despised by the people. All who see me mock at me, they make mouths at me, they wag their heads; He committed his cause to the LORD; let him deliver him, let him rescue him, for he delights in him!

And Annas paused to state, "Did we just now hear you utter these very words, Caiaphas?" Caiaphas even in the darkness turned red. Annas continued:

Yet thou art he who took me from the womb; thou didst keep me safe upon my mother's breasts. Upon thee was I cast from my birth, and since my mother bore me thou hast been my God. Be not far from me, for trouble is near and there is none to help. Many bulls encompass me, strong bulls of Bashan surround me; they open wide their mouths at me, like a ravening and roaring lion. I am poured out like water, and all my bones are out of joint; my heart is like wax, it is melted within my breast; my strength is dried up like a potsherd, and my tongue cleaves to my jaws; thou dost lay me in the dust of death.

And then Annas paused for effect.

Yea, dogs are round about me; a company of evildoers encircle me; they have pierced my hands and feet—I can count all my bones—they stare and gloat over me; they divide my garments among them, and for my raiment they cast lots. (Psalm 22:1–18)

Reciting the psalm had the expected effect. Several members of the entourage inhaled sharply. "Yes, you are correct, Annas," Caiaphas quickly interrupted and in a more conciliatory voice, "but his disciples are not learned men. They will likely not notice the crude similarities of this execution to this psalm. And we need to leave in order to celebrate the feast of Passover," he added hurriedly.

But many other priests and scribes that day remembered the words Jesus had uttered and saw what had happened. "The scriptures have come alive in our presence," several excitedly, but softly, stated to others![41]

Caiaphas and Annas left the crucifixion, as did others. The strange darkness unnerved many, and the hired crowd had no need to stay now that the chief priests had left. Those remaining close by were the Roman execution detail; the condemned men; Jesus' mother, Mary; his aunt Mary, the wife of Clopas; Mary Mag'dalene; and his apostle, John. Many of Jesus' acquaintances and the women who had followed him from Galilee stood at a distance.[42]

"I thirst," Jesus spoke.

A bowl of sour wine was available just for this kind of request and one of the guards put a sponge full of this vinegar on a hyssop[43] and gave it to him to drink. Jesus drank the sour wine and then said, "It is finished."[44]

Jesus died, and the Earth shook violently.

"Stand your ground," Petronius, the centurion in charge of the detail barked to his men.[45] But this was difficult as the Earth continued to shake and rocks split. The remaining folks beat their breasts.[46]

Petronius looked around at the bedlam. Never before had he witnessed anything even remotely similar to this event——strange darkness, an execution attended by obviously jealous leaders of the Jewish state, a condemned man who forgave his executioners, the promise to a criminal of entry into paradise, and as this Jesus cries out, the Earth shakes? Each one of these events was unique. As a centurion, Petronius had been a part of many executions, but never one like this, he thought. Petronius pondered briefly what was actually going on. Then he praised God and said, "Certainly this man was innocent."[47] He was not sure how he would ever explain this whole strange occurrence to Governor Pilate.

The fear and confusion among the people still remaining at the scene continued as did the shaking of the ground, but then very slowly it subsided and the sky began to clear. Within the hour, the crazy events of the execution had all but ceased.

Petronius knew from Jewish custom that leaving the condemned men on their crosses over the Passover was a severe insult, and because his orders also included appeasing the Jewish leaders, he ordered his guards to break the legs of the men to hasten their inevitable death. This was accomplished with its accompanying muted shrieks of pain from the criminals on either side of Jesus, but when the guards got to Jesus, one of them exclaimed to Petronius that Jesus was already dead.

Petronius grabbed a lance, strode over and pierced the side of Jesus with the lance to make sure. The blood and water that rushed out confirmed that the execution was complete, but Petronius, careful as he was, also got splashed with the blood. An immediate feeling of calm and peace overcame him. What is this feeling? he thought. Looking up at the disfigured face of Jesus, he was jarred by an oddity that he at first could not place. Then it occurred to him what the incongruity was. Despite Roman torture that left the strongest men whimpering—and many strong men had whimpered because of Petronius—Jesus' face denied what the marks on his body plainly stated. In contrast to his body, the face of Jesus was serene.

How could this be? Petronius asked himself. Tortured beyond human endurance, profuse bleeding from wounds all over the body, including all around the head, and this Jesus is, what, smiling? Well, not smiling, Petronius thought, more like satisfied. No human could endure this and be satisfied. Petronius exclaimed, "Truly this man was a son of God."[48]

> [And] the heavens [told] the glory of God; and the firmament proclaim[ed] his handiwork. (Psalm 19: 1)

The sun came out after the death of Jesus. The

constellation Ram was clothed[49] in this sun. The Ram, the sacrificed Son, had returned to the Sun, the Father.[50] This, the second of the three heavenly signs, was present for all to witness.

———— ◊ ————

Pilate was surprised at the early death of Jesus. He was even more surprised at his next visitor, Joseph of Arimathe'a from the Sanhedrin, who asked for the body of Jesus.[51] It was just as I had thought, Pilate mused. The chief priests and his cronies had trumped up some charge against this Jesus and not everyone had agreed. He consented to the request at once.

———— ◊ ————

Caiaphas and Annas were just past the gates into Jerusalem as the earthquake occurred, and it threw many of the entourage down to the ground. It was only with a great effort that the carriages carrying the high priests did not tumble. The Earth shook a long time. Afterward, the entourage reassembled, made sure that everyone was unharmed, and then proceeded. But soon a messenger reached them to report a temple disturbance.

"Your holiness, I apologize for bringing you bad news, and you may find this is hard to believe, but the temple's curtain, the very one that separates the presence of God from his people,[52] has been torn in two, from top to bottom."[53]

"What? Who has done this?" shouted Caiaphas, and he urged his porters to hurry back to the temple to investigate this outrageous event, Annas, in contrast, stayed behind with his porters.

Annas got out of his carriage and sat down on a boulder by the road in a daze, his head a swirl of thoughts. He sat for over an hour. Later, as the sun began to set, Annas got up to attend the Passover feast. He looked east and saw the Passover moon on the rise…in eclipse—a blood moon. Annas started to shake, as the words of the Prophet Joel came to his mind in a rush:

> The sun shall be turned to darkness, and the moon to blood, before the great and terrible day of the LORD comes. (*Joel: 2:3*)

Joel's prophesy is unfolding in front of my eyes, Annas thought, and then his thoughts continued, My God, all of these prophecies have passed before my eyes today…. I should be happy. But Annas was a miserable man.

"What have we done?" he exclaimed as terror built up within him. He thought, If Joel was correct, then the great and terrible day of the Lord was to quickly be upon them, but he did not know what this could be. And as his terror overtook him, upon this now third heavenly sign, he quickly sickened and threw up by the side of the road what little remained of his lunch.

End Notes

[30] For additional insights into Simon of Cyrene and his two sons, please see Early Libyan Christianity: Uncovering a North African Tradition by Thomas C. Oden, InterVarsity Press, Downers Grove, 2011.
[31] See Mark 15:21.
[32] See Matthew 27:4.
[33] See Matthew 27:5–8.
[34] See Luke 23:27–28.
[35] See Luke 24:20.
[36] See Matthew 27:45; Mark 15:33; Luke 23:44. Darkness was the first of 3 signs that the heavens prepared to announce the death of Jesus and the kingdom of God.
[37] This insight is from Solomon's Temple at http://www3.telus.net/public/kstam/en/temple/details/day_of_atonement.htm, which quotes the following scripture.
He shall take the two goats and present them before the LORD at the doorway of the tent of meeting. Aaron shall cast lots for the two goats, one lot for the LORD and the other lot for the scapegoat. Then Aaron shall offer the goat on which the lot for the LORD fell, and make it a sin offering. But the goat on which the lot for the scapegoat fell shall be presented alive before the LORD, to make atonement upon it, to send it into the wilderness as the scapegoat. (Leviticus 16:7–10)
[38] See Luke 23:34.
[39] See Luke 23:42–43.
[40] I owe a huge debt of gratitude for this insight to Fulton Oursler and his book The Greatest Story Every Told (page 338). Mr. Oursler goes on to write a chapter (page 340) about the aftermath of the crucifixion and

resurrection from the viewpoint of Annas and Caiaphas that is fascinating. I highly recommend reading his book.

[41] And the word of God increased; and the number of the disciples multiplied greatly in Jerusalem, and a great many of the priests were obedient to the faith. (Acts 6:7)

[42] See John 19:25 and Luke 23:48.

[43] John's reference to "hyssop" in this passage was intentional. It refers back to its first use in the Bible during the Exodus sage of Israel. "Take a bunch of hyssop and dip it in the blood [of the lamb] which is in the basin, and touch the lintel and the two doorposts with the blood which is in the basin; and none of you shall go out of the door of his house until the morning. For the LORD will pass through to slay the Egyptians; and when he sees the blood on the lintel and on the two doorposts, the LORD will pass over the door, and will not allow the destroyer to enter your houses to slay you." (Exodus 12:22–23)

[44] See John 19:28–30.

[45] See Jesus and the Eyewitnesses by Richard Bauckham (William B. Eerdmans Publishing company, Grand Rapids, Michigan) in which he gives reference to name of this centurion in the Gospel of Peter 8:31.

[46] See Matthew 27:51 and Luke 23:48.

[47] See Luke 23:47.

[48] See Mark 15:39.

[49] What does it mean to be clothed in the sun? Walk outside on a cloudless day during daylight hours and what do you see in the sky besides the sun? Unless the moon is at least partially full, you will see only blue skies and the sun because the sun's light is so overpowering as to "clothe" all other lights in the sky. And, assuredly, many other lights are there, as more than amply demonstrated during a solar eclipse when the sun's light is blocked by the moon. On April 3, 33

AD, the constellation the Ram was clothed in the sun, which occurs yearly over a period of several weeks.
[50] One of the more remarkable occurrences of the crucifixon of Jesus is the location. Golgotha is thought by some to be the location of the near sacrifice of Isaac by Abraham in the Old Testament (see https://en.wikipedia.org/wiki/Binding_of_Isaac). Instead of sacrificing Isaac, however, God provides a ram. (Genesis 22:24)
[51] See Luke 23:50–52.
[52] This curtain separated the Holy Place from the Holy of Holies. The Holy Place was attended twice a day by priests chosen by lot. The Holy of Holies was attended only once a year, on the Jewish Day of Atonement, and only then by the chief priest.
[53] See Matthew 27: 51; Mark 15:28; and Luke 23:45.

Chapter 5

Into Hell

Saturday, April 4, 33 AD, Passover in Jerusalem

Pilate was surprised once again when the chief priests and Pharisees gathered before him in the morning, and on their high holiday at that, asking for a guard on the tomb of Jesus. Caiaphas explained:

> *Sir, we remember how that imposter said, while he was alive 'After three days I will rise again.' Therefore, order the sepulcher to be made secure until the third day, lest his disciples go and steal him away, and tell the people, 'He has risen from the dead,' and the last fraud will be worse than the first. (Matthew 27:63–64)*

Pilate thought, this is ridiculous. Everyone knows that stealing bodies or anything else from tombs in

Caesar's realm is strictly forbidden and severely punished.[54] But once again, Pilate acquiesced to their unusual request. First a rigged trial and now a Roman guard, he thought, and coming to me so early on their most holy day must have been hell for them, he chuckled. However, it was their holy day, so appeasing these locals would be expected. Pilate order Petronius to take a contingent of soldiers and stand guard.

Passover was without hope for the many people in Jerusalem who had clung to the words of Jesus during the week leading up to the feast. This was especially true for his long-time followers. Not one of them had eaten the feast, nor conducted the ceremonies, nor sung songs, nor recited any prayers the previous evening. The pain and despair of seeing Jesus crucified—and being unable to do anything about it—was searing. The events of the day before—the unearthly darkness between noon and 3 p.m.,[55] the earthquakes, the report of the temple curtain being torn in two, the testimony from a centurion, the leader of the crucifixion team no less, that Jesus was a son of God—never had such a day as this been experienced by anyone. And then, as the sun set and Passover was to begin, the full moon, rose in the East in eclipse—a blood moon! What did this mean? they all wondered. It had been a horrible Friday. Passover started out even worse, and now, Saturday, the Sabbath, was despair.

The disciples of Jesus stayed together in the house where they had their last dinner together. I denied him three times, Peter thought, and then his jumbled thoughts continued, a victory for Satan…It could not be any worse than this… Judas hanged himself... What am I to do?

Not one of the remaining disciples, or any of the many women who administered to Jesus' itinerate group, said much to each other all during the Passover day. John, the only male disciple to witness the crucifixion and all the sordid events afterward, despondently relayed several of Jesus' last words to the group, seemingly over and over again, but this was nearly the extent of the conversation.

John kept replaying in his mind the last supper, and the ensuing betrayal, arrest, trial, conviction, beatings, scourging, insults, sentencing and agonizing death. WHY DID IT HAVE TO END IN THIS WAY? John kept thinking. If Jesus was truly the Messiah, as he and others fervently believed, how was this part of God's plan of salvation?

The only consolation during this hellish Passover day appeared to be a happenstance. Simon of Cyrene had been forced by the Romans to carry the crosspiece of Jesus on that sorry walk to Golgotha when Jesus faltered.[56] Simon, overcome by this unwanted assignment, nevertheless stayed with his two sons to witness the crucifixion of Jesus from a distance because of Jesus' comments to him along the way.

It had been a wretched spectacle. Afterward, one of the women had invited Simon and his sons to stay over with the larger group of Jesus' followers to "celebrate" the feast of Passover, not that anyone celebrated.

Sometime during the afternoon, Simon told the group that he had come to Jerusalem with his sons specifically to find Jesus, but he had been a most unwilling volunteer and loath to be a part of Jesus' crucifixion. As Simon relayed his reasons for coming to Jerusalem to meet Jesus, the group soon realized that he was a magus, and not just any magus, but one time apprentice to Gaspar, one of the same magi that they had visited Jesus, Mary, and Joseph a short thirty-three years in the past.

The message was captivating. Mary, the mother of Jesus, grew quiet as she looked at Simon, and then nodded her head in agreement. Yes, this was Simon, the very excitable apprentice of Gaspar, whom she had met under glorious circumstances at Jesus' birth. He has aged well, Mary thought, and his sons are a delight, even in this trying time.

Mary and Simon embraced, and the mood lightened. Simon then told all of Gaspar's prophecy, that he, Simon, would somehow be able to help Jesus on his mission for our salvation. No one, not even Simon, however, knew what this meant. And then Simon reluctantly brought up the other prophecy, that of Daniel, one of the revered Jewish ancestors and the head of the Jewish sect of magi from Babylonian time. Simon said, "Daniel predicted that the anointed one,[57] the Messiah, your—our— Jesus, would be cut off, or killed, at around this time."

No one spoke to this revelation, and the group fell slowly again into a disquiet.

Sometime later John exclaimed, "Not a bone in his body was broken."

Several others exclaimed angrily that that was well and good that Jesus was already dead on the cross because the act of breaking the legs of the crucified with a bludgeon to hasten their death due to asphyxiation was too painful to even contemplate.

"So what?" Peter asked.

But John was not paying attention. "And he died at the time of the sacrifice of the lambs for Passover." John continued, not really to anyone in particular.

"Of course, he did," Peter spat out. "Why does this matter?"

James then said, "'He keeps all his bones; not one of them is broken.'[58] John," James continued, "what again did Jesus say while hanging on the cross?"

"Not many things," John responded, "Why do you ask again?"

"You mentioned earlier his cry out to God."

"Yes," John replied, "Jesus said: 'My God, my God, why hast thou forsaken me?'"

"The beginning of Psalm 22—My God!" exclaimed James, "This is just what happened." And after a pause, during which no one seemed to even breathe, James continued:

> *All who see me mock at me, they make mouths at me, they wag their heads; He committed his cause to the LORD; let him deliver him, let him rescue him, for he delights in him! Yea, dogs are round about me; a company of evildoers encircle me; they have pierced my hands and feet—I can count all my bones—they stare and gloat over me; they divide my garments among them, and for my raiment they cast lots. (Psalm 22:7–8; 16–18; Luke 23:35; John 19:24)*

Mary, the mother of Jesus, and the other women who were at the crucifixion nodded their heads in agreement with John, and many started to weep once again.

John, struggling to understand, said, "At our last supper, Jesus said "for I tell you that from now on I shall not drink of the fruit of the vine until the kingdom of God comes."[59] John paused in thought.

James encouraged him, "John, please continue; you alone among our apostles was there yesterday. Do not let your youth keep your thoughts from us, son of thunder."

John continued, "Yesterday, on the cross, before he died, Jesus said that he thirsted and then drank the sour wine that was offered. He then said, 'It is finished,' and died."[60]

"But what does this mean?" asked Peter, but this

time in a tone of contemplation.

After a lengthy pause, James replied with a question, "Jesus drank the fruit of the vine again, so has the kingdom of God come?" And after yet more time, James continued:

> *Now is the judgment of this world, now shall the ruler of this world be cast out; and I, when I am lifted up from the earth, will draw all men to myself.[61] (John 12:31-32)*

"So the kingdom of God has come," stated Peter matter–of–factly. "But what does this mean?" No one responded.

Evening came, and when the sun set and Sabbath was past, Mary Mag'dalene; and Mary, the mother of James; and Salome, a fellow disciple went out and bought additional spices so that they might go and anoint the body of Jesus the following morning.[62]

End Notes

[54] The disturbance of graves and tombs in the first century was a capital offense (Rodney A. Whitacre. John. InterVarsity Press, Downers Grove, Illinois. page 472).

[55] Between the sixth and ninth hour; see Matthew 27:45.

[56] See Mark 15:21.

[57] See Daniel 9:26.

[58] See Psalm 34:20.

[59] See Luke 22:18.

[60] See John 19:30.

[61] The author was in Jerusalem during November of 2016. Outside the chapel on the Via Dolorosa devoted to Jesus stumbling, he heard inside the singing of the hymn "Lift High the Cross" in English. Presuming that the group inside was from nations who spoke English, he was surprised to see who filed out of the chapel after the song ended: Asians, Africans, South Americans, and Europeans of various nations, and yes also folks whose native tongue was English... Indeed, Jesus had drawn all "men" to himself.

[62] See Mark 16:1. The word "additional" seems appropriate here because Luke 23:56 suggests that at least some spices and ointments were available on the day of the crucifixion.

Chapter 6

---◆---

The Great and Terrible Day of the Lord

The sun shall be turned to darkness, and the moon to blood, before the great and terrible day of the LORD comes. (Joel 2:31)

Sunday, April 5, 33 AD, the First Easter

An intense radiation filled the body of Jesus.[63] He woke up and arose through the Shroud,[64] leaving behind a mixture of myrrh and aloes, and arrangements of flowers. Looking back at the limestone ledge on which he had rested, he saw the linen napkin, which had been place on his head on the way to the tomb to honor Jewish sensibilities.[65] It was rolled up and placed separately from the Shroud. He left the Shroud as it lay. He did not remember being laid in it, but of course, he had already died by then.

Whoever buried him in this limestone cave must have done so in haste because not much time had remained between his death and sundown[66], and the start of the Jewish Passover, two evenings earlier.[67] But even so, whoever buried him had followed the proper procedure for a Jewish man dying a violent death,[68] adding the mixture of spices, laying flowers, and then placing his body in the Shroud and, to its side, the linen napkin.

Getting permission to even bury a crucifixion victim was most unusual. He wondered who did this, and then smiled. It was likely either Joseph of Arimathe'a or Nicode'mus, both from the Sanhedrin. Both of them were in anguish during his Jewish trial, and at least Arimathe'a had not consented to his conviction of blasphemy.[69] Nicode'mus had even argued that if Jesus were the Messiah, then his answer would be entirely appropriate, and that otherwise how could the Sanhedrin make this determination. "Are we not looking for the Messiah?" he exclaimed loudly. But of course, their anguish had been in vain. Jesus had been convicted.

However, either or both of these men would have had sufficient standing before Pilate to ask for his body, and Pilate would be inclined to comply. Pilate had tried to prevent the crucifixion in the first place.[70]

It was going to be a glorious morning in Jerusalem. Jesus stepped out in it, noticed the Roman guards lying around in a stunned fashion, and briefly worried about what would become of them when it became known that he was no longer in the tomb. He could imagine the chief priests and Pharisees asking Pilate about posting a guard.[71] He offered a brief prayer on their behalf and then walked into the early morning predawn, smelling the freshness of the dew and the scent of Anthemis flowers,[72] and breathing in the ever-present pollen that was continuing the life of so many plants.

———◇———

It had been a listless night and few of Jesus' disciples had slept. At early dawn, several of the women who had come with Jesus from Galilee, gathered the additional spices they had purchased the previous evening and left for the tomb of Jesus with the intention of making a more complete preparation for his body. However, when they came to the tomb, they found the stone rolled away.[73] So leaving the other women, Mary Mag'dalene ran, and went to Simon Peter and the other disciple, the one whom Jesus loved, and said to them:

> "They have taken the Lord out of the tomb, and we do not know where they have laid him."
> Peter then came out with [John], and they went toward the tomb. They both ran, but [John] outran Peter and reached the tomb first; and stooping to look in, he saw the linen cloths lying there, but he did not go in. Then Simon Peter came, following him, and went into the tomb; he saw the linen cloths lying, and the napkin, which had been on his head, not lying with the linen cloths but rolled up in a place by itself.[74] Then [John], who reached the tomb first, also went in, and he saw [the image on

the linen cloths] and believed [in the resurrection]; for as yet they did not know the scripture, that [Jesus] must rise from the dead. Then the disciples went back to their [meeting place].[75]

But Mary [Mag'dalene, after returning,] stood weeping outside the tomb, and as she wept she stooped to look into the tomb; and she saw two angels in white, sitting where the body of Jesus had lain, one at the head and one at the feet. They said to her, "Woman, why are you weeping?" She said to them, "Because they have taken away my Lord, and I do not know where they have laid him." (John 20: 2–13)

Jesus returned from his walk and noticed that the guards were no longer there, but that someone was weeping outside of his former tomb.

[Mary Mag'dalene] turned round and saw Jesus standing, but she did not know that it was Jesus. Jesus said to her, "Woman, why are you weeping? Whom do you seek?"

Supposing him to be the gardener, she said to him, "Sir, if you have carried him away, tell me where you have laid him, and I will take him away."

Jesus said to her, "Mary."

[Recognition set in] She turned and said to him in Hebrew, "Rab-bo'ni!"[76]

Jesus said to her, "Do not hold me, for I have not yet ascended to the Father; but go to my brethren and say to them, I am ascending to my Father and your Father, to my God and your God." Mary Mag'dalene went [to the meeting place] and said to the disciples, "I

*have seen the Lord", and she told them that he
had said these things to her. (John 20: 14–18)*

The other women who went to the tomb with Mary
also said that they had seen both angels and Jesus.[77] But
the disciples did not believe that any of the women had
seen Jesus,[78] even after both John and Peter acknowledged seeing the empty tomb. Mary Mag'dalene
smiled. It did not matter. The joy in her heart was
overwhelming. She had seen the Lord, and the thought
of her encounter with Jesus thrilled her senses. And for
the rest of the morning, Mary and the women who had
seen Jesus and the angels were ecstatic.

John had shown the linen cloths, one with the image
of Jesus' body, to everyone with the statement that since
this image was not made by human hands, looking at
the image on the cloth was not forbidden. James agreed
and everyone looked. The apostles were disgruntled,
however, wanting to believe, but incredulous that Jesus
would first appear to women, and not them. Simon of
Cyrene and Mary, Jesus' mother, spoke quietly together
about what the next event for the kingdom would be, if
the women were correct that Jesus was alive. Secretly,
however, Mary knew that Jesus was alive. For how
could her son, the Son of God, not be!

During the late morning, reports of the empty tomb
were circulating throughout Jerusalem and Jesus'
disciples were being blamed for stealing his body.[79]
Petronius had reported seeing some of Jesus' disciples
at the tomb in the early morning. The burial cloths had

disappeared. Reports that the temple curtain had been torn in two were also whispered among the shops.[80] Some people even reported seeing their dead loved ones walking around the streets of Jerusalem. Fear of the authorities gripped the apostles and disciples, and they locked the doors where they were staying.[81]

Just after noon, Peter said to James, "I am taking a walk, I need to get some air."

Stepping out of the locked room, Peter moved along the busy streets unnoticed. Turning a corner, he ran into a person whom he did not immediately recognize.

"Peter," Jesus said.

Peter stepped back. "Lord?" he stammered. A bliss rose in his chest to such an extent that he thought it would burst. Then a torrent of shame filled his face, and he fell to his knees. "Lord, I am not worthy to be called one of your disciples. I am such a sinful man."

Jesus replied, "Simon, it was necessary for me to suffer these things before I entered into my glory.[82] But now, go back to your fellow followers and let them know you have seen me. It is important for them to be encouraged."

Peter's overwhelming feeling of remorse lessened at these words. The Lord still loves me, he thought. Looking up to acknowledge his task, he noticed Jesus was gone.

The upper room was abuzz with conversations, nearly as many as there were people in the room. Peter's announcement had the expected effect—

encouragement! Afternoon wore into evening, and the uneaten Passover feast of the prior day was gladly and heartily eaten now. Suddenly, a disciple of Jesus, Cle'opas and his companion who had left the group earlier in the morning burst back into the room——with the news that they had walked and talked with Jesus on the way to Emma'us, seven miles away from Jerusalem.[83]

"He explained the scriptures to us and how he fit into them," Cle'opas waxed enthusiastically. "Yes," his companion continued, "I was particularly surprised at his teaching of Isaiah 53."

Everyone looked at James.

"Well, yes, Isaiah 53, do you all want for me to recite this?" James asked of no one in particular.

"James, for a man of vast knowledge, you sometimes ask dumb questions. Of course, we do!" exclaimed Peter.

"Well, Peter, I appreciate your compliment, right? Well anyway, I will recite this chapter for you all, but please, anyone, feel free to correct me if I get parts of it wrong."

Mary, Jesus' mother, smiled and reminisced. Jesus and James[84] would often quote scripture to one another, and this was one of their many favorite passages to argue. James had always maintained that the suffering subject of the chapter was Israel, consistent with the traditional interpretation. Jesus always maintained that the passage applied to an individual, but he never said who he thought that this individual was.

As Mary listened to James, she finally understood why:

> *He was despised and rejected by men; a man of sorrows, and acquainted with grief; and as one from whom men hide their faces he was despised, and we esteemed him not. Surely he has borne our griefs and carried our sorrows; yet we esteemed him stricken, smitten by God, and afflicted. But he was wounded for our transgressions, he was bruised for our iniquities; upon him was the chastisement that made us whole, and with his stripes we are healed. All we like sheep have gone astray; we have turned every one to his own way; and the LORD has laid on him the iniquity of us all. He was oppressed, and he was afflicted, yet he opened not his mouth; like a lamb that is led to the slaughter, and like a sheep that before its shearers is dumb, so he opened not his mouth. (Isaiah 53:3-7)*

And at this, John interrupted, "Jesus did not answer his accusers during his trial." James paused to let John's words sink in and then continued with Isaiah's passage:

> *By oppression and judgment he was taken away; and as for his generation, who considered that he was cut off out of the land of the living, stricken for the transgression of my people? (Isaiah 53:8)*

Not one of us thought this, Peter realized. And then James paused, again, recognizing that the next verse was a direct match for what had happened on Friday:

> *And they made his grave with the wicked and*
> *with a rich man in his death, although he had*
> *done no violence, and there was no deceit in*
> *his mouth. (Isaiah 53:9)*

Several in the group make exclamations of amazement, recalling the thieves who were executed on either side of Jesus and the offer of Joseph of Arimathe'a, a rich man,[85] to inter Jesus in his own grave. James continued:

> *Yet it was the will of the LORD to bruise him;*
> *he has put him to grief; when he makes himself*
> *an offering for sin, he shall see his offspring, he*
> *shall prolong his days; the will of the LORD*
> *shall prosper in his hand; he shall see the fruit*
> *of the travail of his soul and be satisfied; by his*
> *knowledge shall the righteous one, my servant,*
> *make many to be accounted righteous; and he*
> *shall bear their iniquities. Therefore I will*
> *divide him a portion with the great, and he*
> *shall divide the spoil with the strong; because*
> *he poured out his soul to death, and was*
> *numbered with the transgressors; yet he bore*
> *the sin of many, and made intercession for the*
> *transgressors. (Isaiah 53:10-12)*

James finished and then looked at his mother, Mary. "Mother, Jesus was right once again in one of our many arguments. This passage was about him." Mary smiled and nodded in agreement.

> *As they were saying this, Jesus himself stood among them. (<u>Luke 24:36</u>)*
>
> *"Peace be with you," he said. (<u>John 20:19</u>)*
>
> *But they were startled and frightened, and supposed that they saw a spirit. And [Jesus] said to them, "Why are you troubled, and why do questionings rise in your hearts? See my hands and my feet, that it is I myself; handle me, and see; for a spirit has not flesh and bones as you see that I have." (<u>Luke 24:37-38</u>)*
>
> *When he had said this, he showed them his hands and his side. Then the disciples were glad when they saw the Lord. (<u>John 20:20</u>)*
>
> *And while they still disbelieved for joy and wondered, [Jesus] said to them, "Have you anything here to eat?" [The disciples] gave him a piece of broiled fish, and he took it and ate before them. (<u>Luke 24:41–43</u>)*
>
> *Jesus said to them again, "Peace be with you. As the Father has sent me, even so I send you." And when he had said this, he breathed on them, and said to them, "Receive the Holy Spirit. If you forgive the sins of any, they are forgiven; if you retain the sins of any, they are retained." (<u>John 20:20–23</u>)*

Jesus took a private moment with his mother, and then left as suddenly as he had appeared. The whole event with Jesus had lasted only a short time. Gradually the noise in the room from all of the conversations increased. No one seemed worried about being found by the authorities now.

Simon looked around the room in bemusement. How is this even possible? he thought. Just yesterday he and the others were in despair, and it was hard to get anyone to talk. He was sure that Satan had won and that hell had come to Earth. Now the group, his group, had the appearance of a nearly raucous party. Everyone was happy. And why not? he thought, our Messiah has come!

"What a great day," he exclaimed.

James noted Peter's expression and asked, "And what is our big fisherman thinking?"

Peter looked up, "I have never had a crazier day in my life. I wake up this morning with a terrible dream about your brother, Jesus, and then realize it was not a dream. Then Mary Mag'dalene bursts in with her outrageous statement; John and I run to the tomb and find the burial cloths arranged as if they still held the body—but they don't– and the burial shroud has a shadow of our crucified Jesus on the inside; the other women babble on about angels, the rumors spread in Jerusalem about us stealing his body, my glorious meeting with Jesus, Cle'opas' story, and then Jesus again! This started out as a terrible day, but now it is a glorious day...of the Lord!"

"Well, yes," James remarked, "it is a both a great and terrible day of the Lord."

"Yes, great for us, and terrible for Satan!" exclaimed Peter.

And James responded, "Hmm... and just as Joel predicted, it occurred after the sun turned to darkness and the moon turned to blood just three days ago."

End Notes

[63] The most likely radiation was light in the vacuum ultraviolet range (VUV) as more fully described in The Shroud: Critical summary of observations, data and hypotheses. Version 3.0. The Shroud Center of Colorado. 2015, page 71.

[64] This analysis is supported by the radiation fall through hypothesis, which briefly states that the formation of the image on the Shroud appeared to have been influenced by gravity as the body moved through the Shroud in the act of arising. See The Shroud Center of Colorado. 2015, page 71. However, the interested reader will also find fascinating the account by Gilbert Lavoie entitled Unlocking the Secrets of the Shroud, which offers unequivocal evidence that the image formed on the shroud occurred as the body was upright and suspended.

[65] The Shroud Center of Colorado. 2015, page 8.

[66] Assuming that ancient times were similar to current times, this would be at about 7:00 p.m.

[67] Two evenings, but three days according to the way days were counted in these times by Jews. Any part of a day was considered a day. Thus, Jesus was buried before sunset on Friday (day 1), stays in the tomb on Friday evening and Saturday morning and afternoon (day 2 as per the Jewish custom of the start and ending of days), and stays in the tomb on Saturday evening and into Sunday morning (day 3).

[68] See Unlocking the Secrets of the Shroud by Gilbert Lavoie, chapter 4.

[69] See Luke 23:51.

[70] See John 19:12; Acts 3:13.

[71] See Matthew 27:62.

[72] The Shroud has several manuscripts devoted to floral images from plants that were in bloom in April around Jerusalem. The flowers of several of these plants were thought to be placed on the Shroud during the burial of Jesus. See for example: Avinoam Danin. 2010. Botany of the Shroud: The story of floral images on the Shroud of Turin, Danin Publishing, Jerusalem.

[73] See Luke 23:55; 24:1–2,10.

[74] An interesting analysis of this passage by William Nicholson (The Six Miracles of Calvary, Chapter 5, The Undisturbed Grave clothes of Jesus, Moody Press, Chicago, 1928) suggests that the reason "[John] saw and believed" was that the "linen cloths lying" were not only empty but also undisturbed, suggesting that Jesus' body was not stolen, for then the linen cloths would be in disarray or not even there.

[75] Embedded in this scriptural quote is one possible answer to the age-old question of what John saw, and based on what he saw what John believed. The suggested answers are based on a well-wrought argument developed by Gilbert Lavoic (2015, Chapter 10), where he states that since Jews were forbidden to create the image of God or man (as per the second commandment found in Exodus 20:4-6), that if or when John saw the image on the linen cloths, he may have believed it was made by God and not by human hands. Thus, John sees the image, believes that the image is not the creation of human hands but rather made by God, and then believes in the resurrection of Jesus.

[76] ...which means Teacher. One of the reasons John may have put this phrase in here is to dissuade future believers that Jesus and Mary Mag'dalene were lovers. Her response here would suggest otherwise.

[77] See Matthew 28:5–9.

[78] See Luke 24:10–11.

[79] See Matthew 28:11–13.

[80] See Matthew 27:51; Mark 15:38; Luke 23:45.

[81] See <u>Mark 27:52–53</u> and <u>John 20:19.</u>
[82] See <u>Luke 24:26.</u>
[83] See <u>Luke 24:13–27.</u>
[84] This story treats James, often referred to as James the Just, as the blood-brother of Jesus. However, this is by no means certain that James was a blood-brother. He may have been an adopted brother, the son of Joseph before Joseph married Mary, or even a cousin. Wikipedia has a discussion of these various possibilities that appears very credible. See: https://en.wikipedia.org/wiki/James_%28brother_of_J esus%29.
[85] See <u>Matthew 27:57.</u>

Chapter 7

————————◇————————

Dispersal

With few exceptions, the apostles and followers of Jesus continued to use the room of the last supper in Jerusalem as a base of worship and praise after the ascension of Jesus. His followers also had gathered several of his personal items, such as his burial Shroud with an image of his face and body, his headpiece from the burial, and the cup from the last supper, and set them aside as a constant reminder of his life and their continuing work. Other artifacts, such as his clothing at the crucifixion had not been recovered.[86]

Matthew, the disciple who was a tax collector, had used his connections with Roman soldiers and had spoken with members of the Roman guard on Jesus' tomb. From them he learned their version of the resurrection: an earthquake, the blinding continence of an angel, their fear and inability to even move, their unwillingness to go to Pilate afterward, and their eventual payoff by Jewish authorities for their tale of

Jesus' disciples stealing his body.[87] When Pilate heard of this breakdown in his Roman guard, his first thought was for severe punishment. Once again, however, and only by intense Jewish leadership insistence, he looked away from these unusual events. His wife's request to have nothing to do with this just man[88] also played a role in his reluctance to pursue what would otherwise be his normal course of action.

After the Pentecost event, the boldness of the disciples of Jesus was evident to all of Jerusalem and even erudite and respected Jewish elders counseled refrain from attempting to stop this new movement.[89] For a brief time, the growing community of Jesus' followers was tolerated especially while Pilate was still governor. However, shortly after the end of Pilate's reign over Judea, the stoning of the disciple Stephen occurred,[90] and Saul, soon to be the apostle Paul, began jailing the followers of "the way," the early name for the followers of Jesus. This persecution continued until Saul converted to "the way" on the road to Damascus[91] and for about ten years, the church grew in Jerusalem and elsewhere.

44 AD Jerusalem

About that time Herod the king laid violent hands upon some who belonged to the church. He killed James the brother of John with the sword; and when he saw that it pleased the Jews, he proceeded to arrest Peter also. This

was during the days of Unleavened Bread.
(Acts 12: 1–3)

"Peter, we cannot stay here as a group any longer, the persecution is too severe. James son of Zebedee[92] was killed yesterday by Herod Agrippa," said James the Just.

Peter gasped, his heart stricken. James was the first apostle to die and the only disciple since Stephen more than ten years ago. And it was widely acknowledged that Stephen died only because Pilate had been called back to Rome, leaving a power vacuum in Jerusalem—a vacuum that the Jewish leaders capitalized on by stoning Stephen.

"Why? Why is he doing this?" Peter nearly wept.

"Peter, you know full well why this is happening," James countered, barely keeping his composure. "Ever since gentiles have been let into 'the way,' many of our Jewish customs are being disregarded. These people do not honor circumcision, nor our dietary laws. Naturally this causes hostility. And Agrippa was only too willing to make the Jewish leadership happy by killing one of us."[93]

"But it is the will of the Father, and our Lord, and your brother, to preach to these gentiles," Peter countered.

"Peter, you are, of course, correct. Even so, the resentment has been building for many years. Please do not tell me you are unaware of this."

But Peter was aware of it. Since his conversion of the

first gentiles in Caesare'a, when the Holy Spirit fell upon all of them who heard his words, without even being baptized, Jews who followed "the way" of Jesus had been critical of the believing gentiles.[94]

"So where do we go?" Peter sighed in anguish, still struggling to make sense of James's murder, "Is it not the will of the Father for us to continue our work in Jerusalem? Otherwise, how can it be that we bring the lost sheep of Israel into a belief in their Messiah?"

"You may be correct, Peter, but it is still not safe to be here. Perhaps I can stay with a small group of believers and continue to pray for deliverance, but you and others need to leave. After all, did not Jesus also say that we were to go to the ends of the Earth and preach this good news?"[95]

A pounding on the door interrupted their conversation and a contingent of King Herod's guards burst into the room. James protested but was shoved aside. Peter was arrested.

> *And when [Herod] had seized him, he put him in prison, and delivered him to four squads of soldiers to guard him, intending after the Passover to bring him out to the people. So Peter was kept in prison; but earnest prayer for him was made to God by the church. The very night when Herod was about to bring him out, Peter was sleeping between two soldiers, bound with two chains, and sentries before the door were guarding the prison; and behold, an angel of the Lord*

appeared, and a light shone in the cell; and he struck Peter on the side and woke him, saying,

"Get up quickly." And the chains fell off [Peter's] hands.

And the angel said to him, "Dress yourself and put on your sandals."

And [Peter] did so.

And [the angel] said to him, "Wrap your mantle around you and follow me."

And [Peter] went out and followed [the angel]; he did not know that what was done by the angel was real, but thought he was seeing a vision. When they had passed the first and the second guard, they came to the iron gate leading into the city. It opened to them of its own accord, and they went out and passed on through one street; and immediately the angel left him.

And Peter came to himself, and said, "Now I am sure that the Lord has sent his angel and rescued me from the hand of Herod and from all that the Jewish people were expecting." When he realized this, he went to the house of Mary, the mother of John whose other name was Mark, where many were gathered together and were praying. And when he knocked at the door of the gateway, a maid named Rhoda came to answer. Recognizing Peter's voice, in her joy she did not open the gate but ran in and told that Peter was standing at the gate.

They said to her, "You are mad." But she insisted that it was so.

They said, "It is his angel!"[96]

But Peter continued knocking; and when they opened, they saw him and were amazed. But motioning to them with his hand to be silent, he described to them how the Lord had brought him out of the prison.

And he said, "Tell this to James [the Just] and to the brethren. Then he [gathered his belongings] departed and went to another place.[97] (Acts 12: 4-17)

————◇————

Peter departed immediately to Caesare'a, to the home of Cornelius, the centurion whom he had previously converted. Here he found shelter and considered his next course of action. After several clandestine messages with James the Just, Peter then left for Antioch, and because James insisted, Peter took one of the burial linen cloths, specifically the Shroud,[98] and the cup used during Jesus' last supper[99] so that not all of the few remaining relics of Jesus would be in the same place. James kept several other items of Jesus' in Jerusalem, including the other linen cloth, the headpiece, from his burial.[100]

Thus, in the year 44 AD, Peter departed Israel. He stayed in Antioch for seven years, becoming its first bishop and then eventually traveling to Rome where he was later martyred.[101]

However, Peter likely left the Shroud in Antioch. The next series of historical facts[102] that point to the Shroud's existence occurred from about 370 to 410 in artwork that shows Christ with features of a long and narrow face with long hair parted in the middle and a medium-length beard, that was also apparent on the image of the Shroud. Also, the History of Antioch, written by Glanville Downey, refers to "an image of Christ...which was an object of particular veneration" in about this time range.

Unfortunately, in June of 540 Antioch was sacked. The Patriach, Ephraemius, left Antioch and went to Cilicia on a mission to safeguard treasured church objects. A few years after the fall of Antioch the Greek word "acheiropoieta" came into use to refer to images of Christ that were "not made by human hands," and an object bearing an image of Jesus was paraded in the city of Cilicia in 554, nine years after Ephraemius arrived. At about that time, an icon called Christ Pantocrator (a Greek word meaning ruler of all) was also created (see Figure 3 in the Appendix). The historian Hans Belting thinks that this icon reproduces a well-known original at the time of its creation. Moreover, Shroud researchers Mary and Alan Whanger suggest that the icon image and the Shroud of Turin match on more than 150 points of detail, whereas generally 40 to 60 are enough to declare forensically that two facial images belong to the same person. These researchers conclude that the artist could have produced such an icon only by looking at the Shroud itself. Also, at some point around this time, the Shroud appeared to have been taken to the city of Edessa.

Near the year 700, a series of gold coins called Solidus were minted bearing the image of Jesus. They were used until the tenth century. A statistical evaluation of the similarities in these gold coins to the Shroud placed the odds of the coins being based on the Shroud at greater than 99.99 percent.

In about 950, the Shroud was captured from the city of Edessa and taken to the city of Constantinople. This was followed, by 1100, by the development of a new iconographic image of the burial of Jesus that had markings similar to the Shroud we know today. In about 1200, the Pray Codex was painted, again with features found on the Shroud.

The Shroud eventually was captured again when the city of Constantinople was sacked by the knights of the Fourth Crusade, and it was moved to Athens; then Venice; Paris; Lirey, France; Chambery, France; and finally to the city of Turin in Italy, where it is found today.

End Notes

[86] For an interesting story about what happened to the robe of Jesus, please see The Robe by Lloyd C. Douglas, Houghton Mifflin Company, Boston, 1942.
[87] See Matthew 28: 2–4; 11–15.
[88] See Matthew 27:19.
[89] See Acts 4:13 and Acts 5:38.
[90] See Acts 7: 58–60.
[91] See Acts 9:3.
[92] This is the apostle James, son of Zebedee and Salome. He is usually referred to as James the Greater to distinguish him from the other Apostle James the Less,

and also James the Just, from a previous footnote. James, son of Zebedee, was the brother of John, the beloved disciple, and probably the elder of the two.
[93] I owe this insight to Walter Wangerin Jr., Paul: A Novel. Zondervan, Grand Rapids, Michigan. Chapter 18.
[94] See Acts 10:44 and Acts 11:2.
[95] See Matthew 28:1.
[96] The Jewish belief at this time was that after death, the angel or spirit of the person remained with the body for 3 days.
[97] The text is vague at this point and in some ways frustrating. However, this gospel was told at the time when members of "the way" were very much being persecuted. Thus, specific reference to Peter's location may have been with some risk. See, for example, Jesus and the Eyewitnesses by Richard Bauckham, William B. Erdmans Publishing Company, Grand Rapids, Michigan, 2006.
[98] How the Shroud was taken out of Jerusalem is speculation. However, it is reasonable for Peter to be the one to keep this relic of Jesus because he was the senior apostle and the second one to observe it after the resurrection. (John 20:6) See also The Shroud Center of Colorado. 2015, page 8.
[99] How the cup was taken out of Jerusalem, or even if it was, is also speculation. See https://en.wikipedia.org/wiki/Holy_Chalice.
[100] How the headpiece was taken out of Jerusalem is also speculation. However, this headpiece is now referred to as the Sudarium of Oviedo, a description of which, and history of its possible movement, can be found at https://www.Shroud.com/guscin.htm.
[101] The Shroud: Critical summary of observations, data and hypotheses. Version 3.0. The Shroud Center of Colorado. 2015, pages 8 and 9. See also https://en.wikipedia.org/wiki/Saint_Peter.

[102] I am indebted to the Shroud Center of Colorado (2015, pages 7--36) for the string of historical facts throughout the rest of this chapter related to the Shroud.

Chapter 8

Reanalysis

February 2016

An older medical scientist returned home from his day's work at the university, where he was studying the toxicity of a chemical used to slow the development of fires in furniture. He had published a study showing that this chemical caused toxicity at very high levels in animals—the equivalent of fifty to seventy sugar packets per person per day. Other studies confirmed this finding. But actual exposures from consumer products were much lower than this, he thought, and would not cause any harm, even in sensitive people, like his four-year-old grandson, Finn, who had just spied him from across the room and who was even then making a beeline to run into his arms. Besides, he thought as he raised up Finn for a swooping hug, I will take the flame retarding benefits of these chemicals any day because destruction of lives and property by fire was a daily occurrence throughout his country.

He knew that not everyone agreed that this chemical was without risk. In fact, he had read a study in which effects from similar chemicals were seen at current human exposures, but this study had not been repeated. And repetition was important because studies were designed to find a positive occurrence every twenty or so times just by chance. Like flipping a coin and getting five heads in a row, he thought. Not a likely occurrence if done once, but if done all day long, five heads in a row would always show up at some point. He had used this example many times in his teaching. This is why repeating a study was so important for science and also why every scientist knew that any one study could not be used to make conclusions.

After giving Finn another hug, he went to his study to look over his evening's work, that on a very different topic—an array of evidence on the Shroud of Turin. Many of his academic colleagues did not give a second thought to this historical relic, or if they ventured a guess, concluded on the basis of one, well-publicized study of its radiolabeled carbon dating, that the Shroud was a clever forgery from the thirteenth century. However, the other studies of historical evidence did not confirm the radiolabeled carbon dating; rather these studies clearly pointed to the Shroud being around prior to the thirteenth century and that it was even used as a template from which coinage and paintings had been made sometime between 300 to 700 AD.

Hmm..., he mused, so if these two types of evidence were contradictory as to the date of the Shroud, then confirmation one way or the other depended on the rest of the evidence. This evidence summarized by the Turin Shroud Center of Colorado was scriptural, historical, medical, fabric, and image formation. It uniformly pointed to a burial Shroud from near the first century, in Jerusalem, in the springtime. And this evidence was extensive. The weave of the cloth was consistent with cloth used for burials in this era. The blood stains were male type AB,[103] similar to that expected in a Jewish man. The stains from other body fluids and other markings on the cloth indicated a brutal execution including severe flogging with a Roman flagrum. The image also bore a wound consistent with a lance blow to the chest. Unusual wounds were also found to the head, along with a profusion of pollen from a plant known to bloom around the time of Passover and also known for its thorns. Additional pollen on the Shroud was from other flowering plants in the spring in Jerusalem. Smaller amounts of pollen were also found from countries around the Mediterranean Sea. The floral prints on the cloth were not inconsistent with plants blooming in Jerusalem during the springtime of Passover, and their placement on the Shroud would be consistent with Jewish burial practices. The soil on the underside of the cloth was of a particular type of limestone, which was typical of Jerusalem then and still now.[100] And importantly, all of these facts fit into the scriptural description of the crucifixion and burial of Jesus Christ.

This medical scientist was used to controversial findings. Thus, controversial evidence about the Shroud should not be unexpected, he thought. In fact, if all of the evidence lined up in support of the Shroud being from the first century, I'd be even more skeptical.

He continued his contemplation. While historical facts can be used to support one version of history over another, such ideas could not be easily tested. For example, the pollen from the plant associated with thorns might bloom in different locations, or the Shroud might have been open to the outdoors during the springtime in Jerusalem. Then again, he thought, if each of these "facts" were assigned a five percent chance of being on or associated with the Shroud—well, other than the radiocarbon dating—the odds of all of them being on or associated with the Shroud were overwhelming. In fact, this collection of facts would be well beyond a one in twenty occurrence due to chance alone and easily more than what I would need to convincingly argue a scientific position in my medical area of work, he thought.

He watched again a video in which Dr. Donald Lynn made a statement that the overall appearance on the Shroud of the executed man's face was completely inconsistent with the obviously tortured body.[7] This led to some additional quiet reflection and prayer, during which time he picked up the latest issue of Biblical Archeological Review and read a story about an analysis of another Shroud dated to around the first century. This Shroud was heavily decomposed.[104] Something started to bother him. What is it? he thought. Nothing seemed to jell. He stopped his work for dinner.

"Grandpa, why is it we never see baby pigeons? His excitable grandson, blurted out as he opened the door to his study and leapt again into his arms.

"My, my," the grandfather chuckled, "my budding young scientist." He actually knew the answer, but in the wise Jewish tradition, he asked Finn what he thought.

"That's a good question, my little man, what do you think?"

"God makes them full grown to start?" Finn ventured.

"Well, that's possible I suppose, but what else might it be?" he responded.

"I do not know," Finn giggled, "My friend, Pearl, back home thinks that pigeons lay really big eggs."

"Well, Pearl may be right on some things, but not this time. The reason we do not see baby pigeons, Finn, is because they do not leave the nest until they are nearly full grown."

"Then why don't we see their nests?"

"Well, the nest normally falls apart with such big birds in it after a short time."

"Oh, Grandpa, you are so smart."

Well, not really, the scientist thought.

"I can't wait to tell Pearl. I know something that she does not."

Dinner was the usual wonderful affair that the scientist had come to appreciate from his wife, a farmer's daughter turned lawyer, who was also renown for her cooking. The day's news was dreary, however. Why don't we ever see good news, he thought. He was tired. His son and daughter-in-law came back, and after a brief, but exciting conversation about their day's events, everyone retired to their respective bedrooms. And as he and his much better half settled in for sleep, his puzzlement earlier in the day briefly arose about the two different shrouds from the first century, but again without any clear picture of what this puzzlement might be.

He awoke in the middle of the night, sat straight up in bed, his mind churning with the evidence of the day before. The unknown insight beckoning him to further thought. Baby pigeons don't leave their nest, Finn, and dead bodies don't leave their Shrouds. Pigeon's nests decay quickly, Finn, and so do Shrouds wrapping a decaying body.

So why is it that we are even able to study this Shroud of Turin?

He briefly encapsulated the facts of the case. Unlike what would be expected from holding a dead body for nearly any length of time, this Shroud was well preserved, with pictorial markings of a crucified male.

Although the dating of this artifact was a problem, it nevertheless contained evidence of an execution that occurred during the spring of the year in Jerusalem. The brutal execution shown on the Shroud was also consistent with the historical accounts of the execution of Jesus.

So why is it that we are able to study this Shroud? the scientist again asked himself. Because the body did not stay in it for any length of time, was his own response. In a swirl of thought, the scriptural, historical, medical, botanical, and geological evidence collectively fit into only one pattern, and pointed him to only one conclusion. And with a sigh of joy he exclaimed…

…Jesus is risen!

End Notes

[103] See Wikipedia, Shroud of Turin:
https://en.wikipedia.org/wiki/Shroud_of_Turin.
[104] For evidence of another Shroud from this era see:
Carney D. Matheson, Kim K. Vernon, Arlene Lahti, Renee Fratpietro, Mark Spigelman, Shimon Gibson, Charles L. Greenblatt, Helen D. Donoghue. Molecular Exploration of the First-Century Tomb of the Shroud in Akeldama, Jerusalem. PLoS ONE, 2009; DOI: 10.1371/journal.pone.0008319.

Epilog

In 1978 a large team of researchers went to Turin, Italy to study the Shroud of Turin. This team was given more than five days of access to examine the Shroud and collect data. The result of this examination and subsequent data analysis can be found in the manuscript The Shroud: A critical summary of observations, data and hypotheses, from the Turin Shroud Center of Colorado, under the auspices of the Shroud of Turin Research Project (STURP). This tome lays out evidence in the following areas: historical, medical forensic, fabric analysis, image characteristics, image formation hypothesis, image characterization, and dating of the Shroud.

Wikipedia also has a vast amount of information on the Shroud, much of which seems well researched. See, for example, https://en.wikipedia.org/wiki/Shroud_of_Turin. However, a web search will also uncover any number of websites that offer credible, and sometimes conflicting, information. Such is the life of a walk in either science or faith or both.

Appendix

Figure 1. Shroud image. On the left is the "negative" image as seen on the Shroud; on the right is the photographic image as developed from the left. Notice that the hair appears to fall straight down as if the man in the image was standing up, and that the shadows on the face indicate that the available light was from above. (Photo credit: Dianelos Georgoudis)

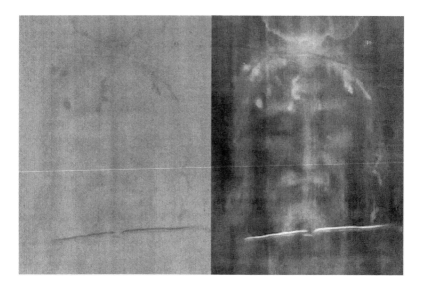

Figure 2. Time line of John and Jesus. Source: http://www.neverthirsty.org.

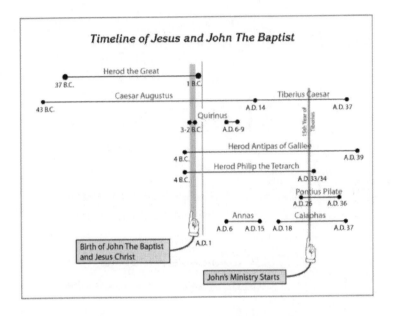

Figure 3. The Christ Pantocrator of St. Catherine's Monastery at Sinai is one of the oldest Byzantine religious icons, dating from the sixth century. See https://en.wikipedia.org/wiki/Christ_Pantocrator_(Si nai)

"Linen Cloths" Study Guide

Several ways exist to approach a study of the Shroud. One way is to read the several Biblical passages devoted to its description, specifically:

- Matthew 27:59–60
- Mark 15:46
- Luke 23:53; Luke 24:12
- John 20:3–10

Also, many folks have written about these descriptions, and several of them comment on John 20:3-10. For example, William Nicholson's The Six Miracles of Calvary, Chapter 5, The Undisturbed Grave clothes of Jesus, suggests that the reason "[John] saw and believed" was that the "linen cloths lying" were not only empty but also undisturbed, suggesting that Jesus' body was not stolen, for then the linen cloths would be in disarray. Another very interesting analysis is by

Gilbert Lavoic (2015, Chapter 10), where he suggests that John believes in the resurrection of Jesus because John saw the image of his crucified Lord on the linen cloths.

This story has John actually taking these linen cloths after he and Peter visit the tomb. This speculation has some support since the very next two verses in John (i.e., John 20:11–12) have Mary Mag'dalene weeping outside of the tomb, presumably after Peter and John had left, and as she wept looking into the tomb and seeing two angels in white, sitting where the body of Jesus had lain, one at the head and one at the feet. There is no record of her seeing the Shroud, or linen cloths, however.

Another interesting account of the resurrection, although one without reference to the shroud, is by Matthew 28:1–4. Matthew was the disciple who was a tax collector, and had likely used his connections with Roman soldiers to speak with members of the Roman guard on Jesus' tomb.

Finally any serious student of the shroud will want to look at the research from The Shroud Center of Colorado (2015). This group summarizes observations, data and hypotheses about the shroud in an even-handed way. Also the video on Jesus and the Shroud of Turin (TLC video. Questar. ISBN 1-56855-944-5) is very well done and would lend itself nicely to an hour long Bible Study, after perhaps a week or two of preparation.

References:

Gilbert Lavoie. 2015. Unlocking the Secrets of the Shroud, Chapter 10. www.Amazon.com.

William Nicholson. 1928. The Six Miracles of Calvary, Chapter 5. Moody Press, Chicago.

The Shroud Center of Colorado. 2015. The Shroud: Critical summary of observations, data and hypotheses. Version 3.0.

Acknowledgements

I have been wonderfully assisted by Elizabeth Mackey who provided the stunning book cover, Ellen Dawson-Witt who gave the many necessary edits and suggested revisions that enhanced the story, David Hansen who provided the way-cool logo for Two Books Press that shows a Christian cross superimposed on the symbol for the hydrogen atom, Carol Newsome who manages all aspects of this effort, Reverend Christopher Dourson for spiritual guidance and countless discussions about this and other relevant topics, and my much better half, Martha Dourson, who listened to countless rehearsals and made many suggestions for improvement, as God's spirit moved me to finish this third story.

About the Author

Michael Leonard Dourson has a doctoral degree in toxicology from the University of Cincinnati, College of Medicine. He works as a Professor of Environmental Science in the Toxicology Excellence for Risk Assessment Center at this same institute. He also leads Bible study classes at Mt. Zion Lutheran Church and the Lucas Community Center in Lucas, Ohio, and through this activity, discovered a love of integrating science concepts with Biblical text. The Linen Cloths Jesus left behind is the third book in a series devoted to this love.

Michael is happily married to his first wife, Martha, a farmer's daughter, turned lawyer. They have 3 lovely children, three lovely children-in law, and three grandchildren. Mike now considers himself fortunate to be number 10 on Martha's list of favorite people.

Does science actually support belief in the birth, death and resurrection of Jesus of Nazareth and the creation of the world? Read other books in this series and see what you think.

Notes

Notes

Notes

Notes

Made in the USA
San Bernardino, CA
08·February 2017